The American Poetry Review/Honickman First Book Prize

The Honickman Foundation is dedicated to the support of projects that promote spiritual growth and creativity, education and social change. At the heart of the mission of the Honickman Foundation is the belief that creativity enriches contemporary society because the arts are powerful tools for enlightenment, equity and empowerment, and must be encouraged to effect social change as well as personal growth. A current focus is on the particular power of photography and poetry to reflect and interpret reality, and, hence, to illuminate all that is true.

The annual American Poetry Review/Honickman First Book Prize offers publication of a book of poems, a $3,000 award, and distribution by Copper Canyon Press through Consortium. Each year a distinguished poet is chosen to judge the prize and write an introduction to the winning book. The purpose of the prize is to encourage excellence in poetry, and to provide a wide readership for a deserving first book of poems. *Living Room* is the eighth book in the series.

Winners of The American Poetry Review/Honickman
First Book Prize

Living Room

1925 A.2 Geister zimmer mit der hohen Tür (neue Fassung)

Living Room

Geoff Bouvier

Winner of The APR/Honickman First Book Prize

The American Poetry Review

Philadelphia

Distribution by Copper Canyon Press/Consortium.

Library of Congress Control Number: 2005927797

ISBN 0-9718981-7-0 (cloth, alk. paper)
ISBN 0-9718981-8-9 (pbk., alk. paper)

First edition
Designed by Adrianne Onderdonk Dudden

frontispiece: Paul Klee, Ghost Chamber with the Tall Door (New Version), Courtesy of The Metropolitan Museum of Art, The Berggruen Klee Collection, 1987. (1987.455.16) Photograph © 1986 The Metropolitan Museum of Art.

Contents

3

4

5

6

Introduction

Readers may be voyeurs, but the subtler gifts are not for the fast glancers. Take a good slow second look at Geoff Bouvier's *Living Room*. (The title, of course, refers to more than one kind of object —the biggest room in everybody's house, but also some uncanny animation; not just to two kinds of object—but also to two kinds of concept.) Bouvier's larger enterprise takes room to heart as room to move—and the "almost expressionless mapmaker" means "to go and go." This writings's ultimata all seem intimate; its cataclysms calm.

Boxes of wordspace, the poems work in paragraphs not stanzas. The poetic sub-units aren't lines but phrases, and those phrases don't so much nail meanings as set them in motion, affording a reader plenty of latitude. "To set the sun, even the sun, among analogies" is the claim of a sensibility alert to the ways in which words can slip from one grammatical category into another ("even" becoming a verb); and also to the ways in which evenings and evensongs, sunsets and stage-sets, nature and nurture, conspire in poetry. "Phrases offer blossomings: to open things," Bouvier writes, and lets the colon remark a grammar in motion—for "open" is as surely an adjective as it is a verb. So whether flowers are offered to things or to readers is a question that remains open. These poems aren't aiming for decision so much as for coincision.

There's bemused contemplation and quirky materiality in these intellectual landscapes—as though Bouvier were the contemporary offspring of Gertrude Stein and Paul Valéry. "Greedy yet generous, giving to get, subjects exchange with objects for their stillness. In return, we export our gestures to things. An indifference of scarf is whisked to a throat . . .", he writes; and, from the poem "Through the Mind":

Open like a beginner, opener, and inrush of concept! My sanded shoreside hole, *to fill* . . . Seeing winter as a summer for raising snow . . . closer to colors of steel and clouds. White you are an eyeful.

The nothing at the eyehole's center—the white of the black—is very palpable. Bouvier's characteristic mode surveys or supplies a calm surprise: a conceptual structure against which uncontain-abilities crop up. "New Day Heyday" is a canny study of conscience lulled by its apparatuses. "Second Going" begins with the protago-nist in the living room, remote in hand—then moves, through jot-tings at the phenomenal thresholds, toward a vision of the un-responsive Messiah. This Messiah doesn't come to stay. And the protagonist, losing his chance at encounter the moment he in-sists on an exclusive choice ("In or out, I say sternly"), reverts from seer to viewer, having had to settle for the tele: "I press play." (A phrase that's only a literary twist from bless and pray, the ear might well remind us . . .). Like Monsieur Teste at the opera, the skep-tic watches the watcher. It's his etymological birthright.

The book contains a number of peculiarly physical meditations on matters of perspective and time—the distance between a rock and a wind, the moment one century becomes another ("Ron went on living. Jamey, also . . . Bob and Tim, Frank and Nick, all contin-ued breathing . . . Greg, it could be said, functioned and existed un-brokenly . . ."). This millennial meditation, a poem called "Personal Trouble," makes what doesn't happen the real topic—a dreaded or hoped-for millennial event that never arrives. What does persist is a litany of proper names remarking at once the human individual-ity and arbitrariness—and the poem ends: "Not to mention many others who're all fine or naughty people enough—just that we are who we are, and haven't deciphered life's true subject in such a way as to be anyone else, or everyone else, or, most difficult yet, no one at all." Life's true subject! Instead, what befalls us turns out to be not millennial change—but the daily failure to bound beyond our bounds. Being is decanted into beings who, stuck in static selves, attend to the moments, not the momentousness.

But agh! Talking about these poems I burden them with a tendentiousness from which they themselves do not suffer. With virtuoso reversals, switches of vantage, changes of scale, inside-outings, they accomplish metaphysical, not only physical, effects. Letters conspire with matter, markers with makers ("April, and all that precipitates. Delightful shows, light showers, busy raindrops tap like typists, any patter the key to a letter. Skies scroll by in one continuous sheet, typing over, whited out."). In "All Roads Lead" Bouvier says the mapmaker "has figured out a way to trace over the experience of the-traveler-in-the-place, instead of merely the place itself, showing not only where one can go, but where one should go, and not even necessarily to get somewhere, instead to go and go." And so the narrative of a mapmaker whose mature works mystify her critics amounts, like much in Borges and Calvino, to a sort of *ars poetica*.

This is a poet's poet: by that I mean that Bouvier is concerned with the refinement of the instruments of reference, even as he deploys them across the sensory field of daily life. Though the experienced reader will find much to admire in all the poems, others might want to begin with just eight—"The Smith Family Trip," "Second Going," "Personal Trouble," "Organized Philosophy," "No, No, Never Nothing," "Homeless," "The Addresses of the Vitalists," and "If Only They Followed the Parables" (this last a brilliant little rhyparography on escalator trash)—these eight alone are enough to make any reader wake up and take notice. They are Bouvier's bravura performances, both accessible and elegant, both immediate and subtle, both hilarious and serious—poems that can tune the unsuspecting mind for Bouvier's quietly suspecting ways.

For Bouvier's a logophile in thrall to the evidences of the daily, a sayer in the sway of senses and sensations. A poem like "Words Fall Apart" is a love letter to the lithest reader, indispensable to the poetic enterprise. When "museum-goers are charged" it is with "a measurable refinement, like electricity." And because Bouvier is canny about the double charges of a word, he can deploy several senses at once: the audience is charged with what it's charged by. Slow and free is how to understand Bouvier's *Living Room;* and "slow" and "free" are the artist's counterpoise to "fastness" in "The Opening," a sort of soirée where "attention is available and paid for by a grant, from the fastness of things, for the slow ways we free them." When these poems hit home, they move what they address. Bouvier's emphasis on Orpheus as failed listener is no accident: it speaks to poetry itself, which must give voice, not only find one. For the beloved could have been saved ". . . if Orpheus had merely listened for her, if he'd urged her to speak, or better, to sing behind him as they picked their way to the world . . ."

Heather McHugh

The subversive does not necessarily proclaim itself as such from the start. On the contrary, in order to act more surely on the beings and things it defies, it often sides with them unreservedly, to the point of speaking in their name.

In this way, white can topple white into a fatal abyss of whiteness by claiming to be whiteness itself.

—Edmond Jabès

1

Living Arrangement

Overnight, the slowly dripping faucet fills a bowl. Brings a music
to our dreams and water for the morning.

Secrets of Defense

Our ground is kept soft with a kind of water, and we dig it up diligently, turning it over with careful industry. We do this for forces outside, whose engines whirred the ways and nights, in hopes that if they someday scale these high walls, they may land here safely.

How to Become a Member

You may have been born to one of us, but if not, not to worry.

You might approach us dancing, or naked. Or lie down in our busiest areas and refuse to move. If you boycott revered gatherings, begin small congregations of your own. Or presume to belong here quietly, copying patterns of movement and speech.

Regardless of how you enter the community, a most significant condition is our reaction.

We must not be wrested from daily routines. We mustn't feel forced to account for your gestures with anything more than a single, prolonged syllable. If we feel like it. For example, "Hmm."

- idea of belonging - space to have - protection · identity.
- "small congregation of your own"

A Happy Hour

After a day or a few hours of good work done, upon the completion of a difficult effort that felt rewarding in the doing, when it might serve one better to celebrate and forget, and then retire to a bed, to rest, for the next day's good works—instead, some of us look back too soon over what it is that we've done. *Just a peek,* I tell myself, a peek at least, but this progresses from a peek into a glimpse, and onward to a glance, until I lose myself in a stare of unlimited scrutiny, which of course enhances the cracks and spaces and imperfections in things, and eventually expresses how a work of once epic-seeming proportions—like the building of a spacious sturdy house, for example—could in fact be very small, the building of a small wall, and not a whole small wall, really, just a half a wall, and not even a sturdy one, which, if I hadn't looked, might have remained a spacious finished house to me, and helped me find shelter and sleep better.

- what is built · what is recognized
as ownership · Mystery ?, Actual
- World of fancy, imagination, human
creation.

The House in Order

You wanted to build a house? I wanted to build a house. We should not have built a house. We built a house.

We should not have gone into the house. If you went inside, you left. If I went inside, I left. This was our arrangement.

You put dreams inside the house. There was you in golden clothes and rosy colors in the dreams. Also in the house. You put changes also in the house, after I left. You left.

I put changes and ways to look at changes in the house. We lived on different pages in the changes. Also in the house.

We passed each other going to and coming from the house. We drew a line with two sides to it.

If we touched hands, it was too much. We touched hands. It was not enough.

We should not have found ourselves inside a house. We lost ourselves, we found a house. We found a house, we lost the house.

- phrases in motion / more structure of prose-like paragraphs.

7

As It Was Going to Be

The clearest stories, strung bell-like back from inevitable conclusions, light one present moment to its restful end. *When he woke up sober she was gone.* Every story, if it is justified and complete, begins at home—at the end—and then returns, to lead its troubled moment back toward narrative's peaceful place. *He drank to make her leave him.* There are preferences that misdirect such orderly themes— selfish concerns, confusion, laziness, and so on—but they reduce to a single reference, the question of sequence, or rather the question of which sequence alights in storied moments from its own end. *Vanilla, cigarettes, wild almond—her smells—stank into gin.* These end-lights shine through darkness in a pattern of necessity, the lack of alternatives branded "inevitability." *An impression in the bed was left to hold him.* For example: I've begun before suitable ends, have not returned here all the way, did not fly straightly through the futures in reversible order, or not the proper futures, or not decisive ones.

- "inevitable conclusions"
- Sequence of events. as Theme here
- Only an impression returns.
- little bonds.

A Study of the Common Thing

Fluttering around the room on a summer night—those interminable loopings and spastic shifts, thrashing as though racked by random shocks—a moth, in fact, hates to fly. It must be mad relief when the moth lands, resting until a curse sweeps it back up to be used by inefficient wings, and it crashes into screens, drawn to the air as it's drawn to light, unable to stay where it was composed and more secure.

- Amazing simplicity - concision
etched idea.

Keep Writing

On the white sink, Courtenay's lost hairs curl into cursive j's, c's, and 9's. Most days they don't seem to, but today they do, try to spell her something. Something in the wind outdoors too is seeking significance. It has to do with the insistent standing-out quality of flags, that pointed whip of things which are tied at one end only, the way hats scoot ahead of their former wearers who, bending, are chasing them.

It's funny to Courtenay that her lost hairs would doodle at all, much less write things of significance, especially after leaving her head for the white sink, for other exterior spaces.

Most days she isn't, but today she is, bent over, reading them.

Like the Only Living Thing

It's easy—august evening—to rest inside the comfort of this living room, considering an interrupted window of late sunlight, and then, in these eyes outdoors, to find an old friend beyond the wide clarity of the sky. To be breathing, allowed. I'm so at ease that I believe I hear another air, a trophied breath—it seems addressed, unworried, unwinding, unchecked—and I'm seasoned as I season in this curious breeze, drafting over covers of stationary ground and never-returning leaves, just here—half-trembling like the blinds inside my living room.

To Speak

And time for this. Otherwise . . .

Orphaned evening saps into shadows, thanks to the sun's absenting quest for evening light. Turns blue, blue, and the blue becomes you.

Deepening daily listening down the hollows out of volume, with its herald notes from bliss this breezy silence.

Quiet viol acclimations.

A challenge to attention in the guise of the neighborhood enables a monument, moment of our blue blue shell, to extend its physically present *concentration of effects.*

Street-darkness soothing undersides of sidewalk-trees, falling coolness pleasantly from day, past words, require: me not to speak.

— "Turns blue, blue, and the blue becomes you"

12

2

Distant Relations

In the sideyard, a rock's trying hard. The wind's kind of Zen. Between them, a million miles (by analogy) although they're touching.

Builder of a Life

As you sit doing nothing, the remote control goes in your hand and fluorescent light lands on the slackened surfaces of you. There's no race you're in; there's nothing more to win. All is fullness and allowance of the spirit. You sit and sink into the sofa, and your lids rest over your eyes. Not your mind, or the channel, changes anymore. Yourself are heaven, your own escape. The water in the glass by your raised feet has begun to condense, dust in the room mingles with the hair on your legs, and your inches of exposed belly heave.

- "remote control"
- "Yourself are heaven, your own escape"

The Late Stages of a Housewife

Death is not a presence until it will never be again, which is true of most instances that sift away behind memories to darkly govern us.

I have a beautiful new kitchen. I spend my time in baking to distraction. My husband meets me there, on the other side of the house, with a book and a gin that looks like tall ice water.

Waiting is what's consuming, like the kind I've been doing for my life to come around. Only the kids visit, now and then, and I'm otherwise undiscovered.

It's like the more I touch things, the more film we leave on each other, so that now I can't touch things. It's all just film on film.

I hope I've said nothing recently about death.

I have finished a sheet of sugary thick cookies.

— "waiting is what's consuming. like the kind I've been doing for my life to come around."

Savings Plan

To save things, collect them in an unremarkable place—behind a row of history books, in the corner of the garage—where you wouldn't usually look. Then forget about these things completely.

When you remember what you're saving—a photograph of an ex, the fattening candy bars—but forget where you're saving it, you may worry, even curse yourself. But remember how this is your plan, and how the plan is succeeding.

The savings are protected, hidden away, even if you can't find them until many days after a rainy day.

- Reads like a book of what is collected -

Trying Fire

I maintain a furnace where I forge everything that I might forget, including myself. *A hasty note, an unworn ring.* The furnace heats the house, which, in time, is also thrown into it. *My favorite color purple, the distance I have traveled.* Essentially, this furnace heats and melts the facts of my life into a singular white point of pure hot, until it has warmed and refined the very moments I've encountered, *a friend who speaks well of winter, love of inland water, sunsets, the Inevitable,* and my furnace heats the remembersome things, and the neighborhoods and towns and even regions all around, *a vase of yellow flowers turning brown,* and also the me who put everything in there in the first place, including himself. In this way, I might reform my memory unselfishly, *a fear, a body, what I've wanted, what you've told me,* that is to say, counter to myself, for the virtues of heat and calm selves to come.

- "This furnace heats ? melts the facts
of my life into a single white
point of pure hot"

New Day Heyday

It mustn't be the lot of some to act, to play mere actors on one country's worldly stage; I, for one, don't portray doers, nor do I do, because a lot differentiates ways, and my ways don't differentiate. In shorter words, I can't decide.

My analyst has termed this *rigorous paralysis*.

Regardless, I never meet the ones I think "maybe" about. The one sensible compromise arises between air and me, at least the oxygen-part of air, and me.

Instead! Right now, to swivel over, cinch my stomach's creasing weight, and swing two great, foundational feet, pendulous and ponderous, under the bed's top edge, winding up whatever rests —collected leaves of skin, this quiet dust. Or to singe one singing vision searing there—gracious windows one transparents, humble wallspace one bares.

No—a conscience can't manage it.

A Situation

They should leave the kitchen open so that we could be fat and asleep. Instead, we find ourselves awake and talking food because they lock the kitchen after meals. If they did unlock the kitchen for us, true, the kitchen would be empty. But we would be full and happy, and, as it is now, it's we who are empty.

Another suggestion which we should make—were we the kind to register suggestions formally, which we are not (as cobwebs over the suggestion box suggest), rather, we prefer to complain, although, to be sure, in these heights of our complaining, we're really no less than icons of angst and persecution, who notice all wrongs the doubtless world wide (as well as our angelic places to right them), feeling close enough to the divinity to whisper our appeals—concerning the situation, an urgent suggestion: lend us a car with which we might go. We're so tied down.

But after all this time, there's no evidence that our longings will be met, merely answered.

Second Going

So completely unmoved by the dolphins on the television science show am I, numbed almost to tears on my leather sofa, unimpressed by the dolphins' intelligence and creativity, undistressed at their submission to fish-wielding biologists, not agog at their effortless showmanship, so unmoved, numbed, unimpressed, undistressed, and not agog am I, that as the show ends, I lock the door, pull the shades, take up my remote, and stop the VCR to rewind it immediately, so that I may sit through the story of the tedious dolphins again.

At this moment, awkward and gentle, not tentative, the Messiah enters, only a step, then stops and stands. After the surprise, I welcome him. I offer him a beer.

But the Messiah comes no farther. He hovers there in the closed doorway, robed in saffron and maroon, half turned as if to leave, lingering above me. His eyes sweep the room, then rise to the ceiling.

With a series of clicks, the VCR stops rewinding. I want to go back to it, back to the television. But the Messiah near the threshold, between things, uncommitted, toying with the folds of his shroud, makes me squirm and grow expectant. I sense a trace of airs at once spiced and cedary.

"In or out," I say sternly, finally. It's not intended to be mean. I'd prefer his company, if he'd only join me. I might feel justified with the dolphins. But I'm bothered by his silent waiting, as if for some inspiration, there on my periphery.

He's waving, then, as he goes, more to catch his balance than to say goodbye. I notice the door seems more solid after him.

I press play.

3

Myth Gave Birth to Philosophy

What happened when the gods learned that their word wasn't good enough?

After Measure

A layers wind, bracingly, and the other within, can tunnel a wish-
mart.

   Sunday.

   Packet on the back of a trust, an I in it, glades of elves. Crumpled
up the lone (path essential) interest.

   Interred on the stone: a sun-chameleon.

   As to analogy: -ist,-est, -er, then . . .

   The parting identifies: a settle-leaf (falls). The sum of my
identities, asunder, leaves, come tumbling calmly goldly down.

— "The sun of my identities"

Through the Mind

Open like a beginner, opener, and inrush of concept! My sanded shoreside hole, *to fill*.

Whatever founded over grounds, I express a warmer round of difference beyond the themes envisioned *now*.

Meantime, inland, the leaves were leaving. Seeing winter as a summer for raising snow, its lengthy shadowed cool December robes, closer to colors of steel and clouds. White you are an eyeful.

" Whit yn arc an eyeful "

Sestina

"Echoes echo?" Off crimson rock canyons, a voice repeats its first impression, caught inflections making changes.

"*Making* changes? Do echoes echo through revision?" To crimson rock canyons, explication makes for repetition.

"For repetition? Never tending toward correction?" Echoes echo in crimson rock canyons with suggestions.

"With suggestions? Who responds to crimson rock canyons' transformations?" Echoes echo like concessions.

"Like concessions to intention?" Echoes echo. Altered answers fade unmentioned from crimson rock canyons.

"From crimson rock canyons, fresh expressions change conceptions?" I don't know. But even disenchanted echoes echo.

Metaphysical Ground

What one thinks is Silence is all another's able to hear. It's not like whatever drives into the terrifying abyss comes back and makes quiet decisions, protecting us. I'm not even sure those demonstrative tenors realize, if they hear it all, what they were *supposed* to leave out.

So there are times when voices wrest away but haven't "gone" anywhere, the way smoke extends, but strangely, briefly, the body of a cigarette. The essence isn't gained or lost, and redolence, in a sense, remains. I think the sublime choirs must wonder, after they harmonize it all, why we never hear it all here. Why say it's Silence, if the places it has been have been brought to us vociferously, as far as it can tell, in their entirety?

— Objects in space 3, Bent

The Field Clear

I don't know but my dream says no.

 Thinking about work (use the pen) work (use the paper) work (forget the pen) throw away the paper.—Tried to deny it, but the sear-white circle of a moon withdrew. *Withdrew.* Returned and smiled *yes* and was loved, withdrew.

 Your quartered, filling mind goes *through its phases.* You sometimes mind *but when it comes back it's great.*

Reciprocity Effects

I am determined by and will change from a list—
. . . .
. . . .—. . . . . . .
. . . .
. . .—faced evasions . . . .
. . . . .—. . . . .
. . . .
. . .—a fervor:
    " . . . .—*backed* . . . .
. . . .*of* . . . .
. . . .—. . . . .
. . . .*of* . . . ."

Not Pathetic Enough Weather We're Having

Read the trees' confusion. Leaves of green words turn in late October. A sun's frown's funny on warm orange pumpkins. Wherever autumn looks, for confidence, to color, it tries listening over summer's mocking. Hot! Hot! Hot!

But I won't feel for it until winter worries away snow. When a willow-bud shoots up somewhere, north of here, dismaying itself and a field of sweaty February.

I Love You! Archaeological Excavation Reveals

1.

Little unusable map, you'll skin me.

The skyline's the limit, and natural born hair, this lock of which, "Is it something, really something?" I said.

A revelation holds its candle to the city, traveling where it's America enough. To the right shot distance? Or just a vicinity.

Sun colors things western this rise.

2.

So it was that splendid summer before the retrospective, picking up something for the pigeons, bread I guess.

There between the awning and the building lay a blue full inch of sky. In that light how right angles had become a tradition, and every bend in the road *seemed*.

Sunny now, but it's raining under the air-conditioners. Just to hold you in my arms, or thereabouts.

Nestled in the bed all softly next to the point.

Somebody Stop LaSalle

1.

Slated for demystification. Lo! To grasp attention, a past-green
spirited leaf falls.

    Outside-up he hies it, the good long slog through muck and
dust. A pee spells relief.

    Insofar as my head, for comfort I wade with a buddy.

    It's bury-a-body desolate.

    We stretch acceptance.

2.

Whew, she's prompt with endurance. But stingier, my stingray:
you're back-lit and I'm squinting.

    Like totally relating, then going out for tattoos. A future sexual
history of permanent body modification.

    Cobwebs on the handle, a branch across the path.

    To the left and right fantasies.

    Come amok with me.

4

Truth is the Person Who is There

The sky meets the mountain with no further obligation.

Everybody Had a Hat

For some, the most difficult part of the day is the portion that is theirs—the hours that are ostensibly already allotted for them—when there may be many fitting hats to choose from, so to speak, after work, and before obligations to a spouse or to a house or to anything or anyone else, when one can affect a range of facts with one's freedom, and select a suitable hat, why not, to wear, and maybe go out, or go all out, pursuing playful escapes, or instead remain prudent, and think about how to feel the next day, and be sure to maintain sobriety and get something done, like the chores, or practical work on a hobby, for instance, applying finish to an old table in the garage that one hasn't been refinishing, or washing already blackened windows, or exploring dense woods which have caught the attention coming home from work for almost three years now, as though now, every evening, although we feel free *from* worldly connections and obligations, there's hardly a justifiable idea of what we're free *to*.

Fortunate Islands

We don't know what we are or do. The suns and oceans and our sleeps conspire, and wind may seem the hum of them sighing together.

Boom! "You blinked and missed the lightning," thunder said. Ovations turned to showers as I turned my waking head.

I must have dreamt . . .

Last night, straddled over soil either north or south, with one foot planted sayable and one foot planted not, a capital A with arms crossed stood careful, steadfast and graphic, on the alert.

A said, "I began my vigil at the increment of the equinox, to balance between silence and a meaningful index."

Now I move my eyelids and think. And although I don't get this, I too was designed for ignorance.

What is a Subject to Do?

Greedy yet generous, giving to get, subjects exchange with objects for their stillness. In return, we export our gestures to things. An indifference of scarf is whisked to a throat and wraps, in folds more artful and considered than by gravity or wind. For our troubles, the scarf's compliance warms.

Other advances—solar power, the ice cube—roll these royal circuits of the world and us together into practical agreements: beds made, patios swept, people tided one with place.

But sometimes a location objects to its residents: the convalescing presence of Lee, propped by coffee under weather, age, and morning light; the syntax and word choices of Jean, with which there has been wrestling; and a rock awry in the arc of its flinging finding vocal, capricious opinion, "Owwww," thunders Robin. There is no absolute humanism.

The Ethics of Tragedy

Before the landscape insisted on a paved hill, the paved hill with a blue house at the base insists; before people insisted, a tall man with a roving gaze, and a couple walking their black dog, and the panting dog itself, insist; before the weather, implacable merging clouds, the considerable temperature, before they persisted, you exist, where they are merely landscape and people and weather. It's as though anything after you might be taken for granted. Any hill, any house, any person, any you informing any situation: you go ahead, and don't ask the question. Then a driver honks and swears angrily and you wonder why; you stub your toe on the curb and are the victim; it begins to rain but you're not prepared; you curse because the stars, even the stars, aren't for you. And then you notice how the tall, specific man avoided the dangerous car; how the actual couple took stock of the clouds and remembered their umbrellas; how the clouds themselves, which seem so literal, weren't far above the moment with its petty yet consequential concerns. And now might be the time, if you could manage it, in your sublime detachment, to reverse the game, and venture on a fresh path for the rain.

— "now might be the time, if you could manage it, in your sublime detachment, to reverse the game."

Altogether Now

While victims become too weak for their own households, losing good say in mundane decision making, to the points of stripped confidence and slips into alcohol and silence and sleep (not to mention other, more serious, desires and devices), yet there are still others—abusive fathers and insecure older brothers, jealous mothers and bitter friends—who can't believe it when their less fortunate counterparts are suddenly compensated (despite rude efforts to divest them of their self-worth, and to convince them of their absolute stupidity), with inspired insights into the difference and nature of things.

Is this how it has to be, or couldn't life resolve itself into unequivocal subtlety?

Now and again, from various isolated, otherwise desolate rooftops, an issuance—immeasurable truth, authentic singing— pours *through* the very mad ones who've climbed to higher perches, above stiff rows of houses that contained them, as though merely being and living together coerce us to be us, to sing or not sing.

Orpheus Out of Tune

His first shortcomings, and the root of later failures, grew from an inability to trust listening. Orpheus baffled his ears with his own song. Which is to say that when truth arrived, the superior piper, Orpheus' mistake was to face that emblematic music instead of listening to it. They could have ensured Eurydice's safety if Orpheus had merely listened for her, if he'd urged her to speak, or better, to sing behind him as they picked their way to the world.

Revisionary Traffic

One who's leading is knowingly, exasperatingly *something,* as something as it feels to read the words knowingly and exasperatingly, and she justifies the company behind her to her. Either they adjust or waste ample appreciation.

And ample breath, crying or trying to catch her or to pass.

Instead, the sunset-shadows of leaves curve over her fresh sweater. Instead of the cinema of it, her swerve, but they can't look, and anyway she's bedazzling in their vision. And anyway she's in the way, and there's no getting around that.

Who rolls left and back in mazing angled lines all down the road, and starts to fit behind her fuming in her train?

Well, it fell to me to play, "She loves me, she loves me not," with the passersby. They're petals!

The Smith Family Trip

The Smith family loaded up the car, got in it, and set out for Florida. Across Connecticut they played word games and sang hymns. On the George Washington Bridge they talked about the weather and the scenery.

Then the father Smith said something and the mother one judged it. The children leaned into each other's space. It was two against two on the New Jersey Turnpike, and by Maryland it was one against three. For a moment in Virginia it swung to four against none, but one of them was asleep, and it didn't count.

In South Carolina, three were asleep, so the driver couldn't play the radio at an audible level. As it grew warmer, they fought about the windows, up or down. By Georgia, the Smiths were completely silent.

When they arrived, one swam, one slept, one walked, and one read in the sun. They were free to think better of each other, far apart in Florida together.

- "plyed word games + sg hym"

Personal Trouble

Even after the particular events of Saturday, January 1, 2000, into which we'll never venture again, which may or may not include venturing into them here, Ron went on living. Jamey, also, persisted with her life. Bob and Tim continued breathing, and seemed quite fully alive. Greg, it could be said, functioned and existed unbrokenly. Frank and Nick remained examples of consistent consciousness. And as for Matt, it could hardly be avoided: well into the unfamiliar millennium, he maintained a vast majority of the qualities enjoyed by those considered living.

Not to mention many others who're all fine or naughty people enough — just that we are who we are, and haven't deciphered life's true subject in such a way as to be anyone else, or everyone else, or, most difficult yet, no one at all.

5

Reinterpreting the Signs

Private property? No. Fishing allowed.

Organized Philosophy

Our purpose is to provide customers with updates on urgent spiritual issues where a voice can make a difference. We identify key abstractions and supply easy and effective methods of speaking out. You can either call your selected targets FREE every day of the week or we'll send a low-cost, well-argued Resident Correspondence on your behalf.

To seal a prayer to God in your name, check here.

If you would like us to suggest a god-term (or devil-term) for you from our extensive list, including rigorous justifications, check here.

To personally censure Evil, or a devil, check here.

To make a friend aware of the existence of the Good, check here.

To hold humankind itself accountable for its crimes, on an individual level, check here.

To enter your name on a formal petition, either to protest or extol the absurdity of it all, check here.

The Town that Believed Wolf

"The Boy Who Cried Wolf" is indeed interesting for the moral message it conveys—surely a million mothers and school teachers can't be entirely wrong—however, this little fable has, over the years, become the subject of gross misinterpretations on the part of these conscientious teachers and mothers, who evidently use it as a kind of aid, to help frighten children from engaging in behavior that is intentionally misleading. Conventional wisdom states that when we genuinely need help, after too much false alarming, no one will believe us. As if our children needed to be scared, or made to doubt their relations with others; adulthood will do that for them soon enough. It's generally overlooked that there was a township of people who listened to the boy's cries, and they stopped listening precisely when listening would have done them some good. When the wolf appeared, adults in the town were already practicing what we might entitle, without an element of irony, Worldly Ignorance: they knew, or at least they thought they knew, and so they could afford to be unaware. By now the teachers and mothers and others disregard the calls of children, who may justifiably cry out over something, even if only for attention, in this complicated world, which along the due course of things has led to the current conditions that our society shares with its wolves.

No, No, Never Nothing

A distinguished coterie of Cal-Tech scientists—led by the illustrious Drs. Lopez and Barone, through years of preliminary study and theorization (including the much-publicized, though ultimately fruitless, if not disastrous, "Monkey-in-the-Box Experiment" of 1989), financed in large part by three global and impatient corporations, not to mention the good graces of the Deans of Cal-Tech itself, from whom extensive laboratory space and equipment had to be leased and maintained, and from whom a seemingly endless stream of graduate students had earned its degrees and moved on into more lucrative, and perhaps more viable, areas of scientific study— finally ready to conclude six years of experimentation toward the apprehension of Nothing, had come to this, presumably last, end: these prominent scientists now contrived to feed smoke into an empty glass room, to witness any traces of the absence of smoke, thereby substantiating and recording, once and for all, the indisputable form and presence of Nothing.

On the appointed morning, before an assembly of primary investors and distinguished members of the international physics community—including Wasvithanyan Onir, the preeminent M.I.T. Nothing Theorist, the great nihilists Theodore Rainier and his wife Helene, and the Nobel Laureate and Black Hole speculator Devin Jones—Dr. Lopez himself manned the controls of the smoke-filling hose, wearing his best blue suit, but half-casual without a tie, and fourteen men and six women watched as the glass room, which Dr. Barone had built, became increasingly filled with whirling scarves of thick smoke. In the room they saw smoke, a gray opaque, more smoke.

It is believed that only the skeptical adversaries of the good doctors felt anything other than broken and defeated, or indeed angry, at least disappointed, that they had come so far and not seen anything, instead of apprehending Nothing.

Insert Object Here

Uncompromised by isolation or measurement of any kind; not struggled against or defended in the name of a national, personal, or religious hope; not the least bit obscured or lightened by palliative technique; neither marked by name, nor given body, nor set in a single contextual field; inedible, indivisible, and to each human sense indecipherable and unknowable; not in, of, or at all answering to a concept, such as the self, or such as time; and regarding which, or mentioning, making useful, or otherwise afflicting with earthly weight, manifestly falsifies.

Homeless

Carrying out his exile to its end, in the pharmacy that summer afternoon, through a flash of insight too bright to be said to have occurred *to* him, and rather encompassing all that he was, on more levels even than his awareness or sub-awareness or future awareness would ever touch (through an insight so vast, in fact, that it would never come into play in any way concerning his body or consciousness, and yet, as concerns his exile, it was, is, and will be of the essence), Gregg Couviev executed (most completely and concretely, with abandon of all doubt and questioning) a secret love for his very self—because of and despite and in spite of himself, most serenely and securely, and whether or not anyone asked, or whether or not he had done something wrong, or whether he were home, incapable, or healthy, or were alone, or whether in any sense he had noticed this, carrying out to one end in the pharmacy that summer afternoon, to the end of Gregg Couviev—by deftly pocketing a tiny heart-pendant for which he had not paid.

The Altruist

There is an altruist on Logan Street in Denver, Colorado, who is the luckiest person alive.

She is neither this lucky because of the simple and functional, inexpensive, but sizeable apartment in which she lives, nor for that apartment's exceptionally large, as guest's comment, bay windows —with their light, and their admirable view of the often snow-covered and majestic Rocky Mountains—although, to be sure, her living arrangements do appear rather lucky. Nor is this altruist the luckiest person alive because of her health, about which, it might be said, she is rarely given to lament or exult, instead periodically accepting the body's mundane and unpleasant effects—a terrible cold, nasty aches—combating these with stoic rest and regular doctor visits, and thereby enjoying sometimes many weeks of unbroken physical balance, all of which virtually escapes the impression of being real luck, at least until she regards the plights of others who suffer physical maladies far more often or more seriously, in which case her average health does finally shine as a cause to be thankful. The altruist is assuredly not lucky on account of her personal life, assuredly not on account of the aspects of her personal life which pertain to her attempted boyfriends, these aspects being, at best, fairly *un*fortunate, finding her more often than not in the rain, literally, crying with dark hair matted and wet, or at home, alone, by a conspicuously silent phone, or otherwise exploited because of her heretofore alluded to altruistic tendencies.

No. The altruistic woman on Logan Street in Denver, Colorado, is lucky beyond the arrivals of common, everyday luck, lucky also beyond the exceptional and infrequent happy accident, lucky mostly in light of her least doings for others, lucky very simply because this altruist is given to derive a vast and uncomplicated edification—balancing the pushes and forces of a host of other impulses, motivations, and desires—merely on account of giving over her seat in a bus, or for volunteering much time, or from buying even large, quite significant gifts, for no occasion at all, with money she does not really have, which paradoxically becomes, to this altruist, an act of utmost selfishness, according herself good feelings, and thereby providing that all she must do to alleviate the poverty of others, is act upon the immodest needs of herself.

The Opening

Museum-goers are charged, a measurable refinement like electricity, as clouds expand their pores outside and drop till feelings rise. There, expertly guided recordings might be purchased for a nominal fee, or we can talk among ourselves: of the flats and straightaways, a relaxed alienation.

Say hello now over sculptures of potatoes and balloons, not entirely unsuggestive. The champagne colors prophecy perfect garble, where words exist provided for and taken down and piled on a plinth with no inscription to the sun, at least sunward. Past an installation without a bottom, and a preference to be around people who go topless.

So much figures into the head, but I've grown accustomed to foreignness in this land and heart-string, where you are not except abstract in representation, and attention is available and paid for by a grant, from the fastness of things, for the slow ways we free them.

6

A Bee's Advice

Open slowly, little red flower. Out here is the Irrational.

Mission

The oceans are big water and their slightest movements are big. Over heaving swells and deeps to be delivered to an island I remembered climbing trees.

It was dark, starless, but the trees bore doorbells, points of light, a fixed radiant pattern most nights. Nor could we swim entirely, kicking and gasping, mouths above, then below, above again, choking foam. With your hands in the air you held tightly to something—an infant—trying to save it. The infant had wings.

The Last Viewpoint

And here I thought I'd earned an unadulterated adolescence, the sovereign experience, both exception and acceptance, the extraordinary life, my rightful hair a wild mind of its own, this latest skin a transparency, with one heart constant to rhythms beyond me.

But it must have been the same for me, and for each one in his or her serial abilities.

Watch the world outside you spin on sensitive, dividing strings: pink puffs, new bursts, a bluet snipped for all blue flowers, stars, or hearts. Now listen.

Those interesting transpositions—ear-to-mouth, resuscitated heards and hardly-heards, unheard of musings let to sudden voice, then sold full voice—these shifting scores that steal the wordless' first-met ears . . .

They teach us that we'll matter in the end. Not that we don't matter now, nor that we matter less now, only that mattering now occurs strictly in relation to the inevitable fact that we'll matter in the end. Even the rich tones of their voices assure us of this, deeply-fatherly, lullaby-motherly, with hearty, heady accents of some half-forgotten, half-remembered home. Write this down.

If we don't believe them, and if we forget too successfully now what they've given us, then I hear there will be little returned to us in the final relation. So although it's now they who matter, we have to trust, and live worthy of the talents being reserved for us.

Civilization University

Since a difference is always fashionable—so long as it's a *new* difference, *old* differences being the worst kind of affliction, serving almost as a definition of affliction, seeing as how an *old* difference (race, or language, or individuality), being *still* different and not otherwise assimilated or overcome, must carry a harmony with truth that lies beyond us, thereby implying measures of truth which are different from, and, by extension, not available to, the homogenizing mass of humankind—so we might do our best to attain to *new* differences (inventions, communications, modes of conduct and interpretations), by deciphering *old* differences into useful, marketable commodities (the latest fashion, the next diversion), away from old differences and the escapable truth.

The Addresses of the Vitalists

No one can remember how we became isolated in the world, but we're rapt by this experience, and today, if we wander through fields, toward spontaneous trees and rivers' brown touches, under steadfast lines of certain mountains, the landscapes never collapse, as though they'd been drawn on horizon-sized paper. And moving away, into unleveled hills, according to our directives, these natural splendors never flatten to a picture. They won't become blotchy greens daubed under a higher blue splinter, one-dimensional, with a single perspective.

The sovereigns, overseeing the way of our times, have specified this phenomenon, and, in the interest of dominion by observation, they've ordered the construction of advantageous places—framing windows and streets, towering parlors for aesthetes—where wide vistas, receding, satisfy our need for appraisable beyonds.

It's All Right Here

He led me inevitably up a mountain he had climbed before—this time with an extravagant purpose, one reason for him and another for me. On the first hand, he said I'd enjoy it, and on the other, he said he wanted to see what he'd become used to, through a new set of eyes.

As we bent to the rugged top and raised ourselves, he smiled and spread his arms for the green heights loping below us, through the haze of the stray highs bluing around us, and he faced me and awaited his surrogate reaction.

"Tough . . . climb," I panted.

Undaunted, his arms extended wide, he burst open all of his awe and accounted me.

The pressure in my temples seemed preposterous in that air.

All Roads Lead

A prestigious map-maker, whose early work was esteemed by travelers—pilots, drivers, back-country anglers, professional hikers, deep wilderness guides—recently began developing an altogether different type of map. This, naturally, exposed the map-maker to intense criticisms, not to mention that her persistence in the matter is proving rather unfavorable for business.

But, in all truthfulness, these worldly concerns never trouble the almost expressionless map-maker. Instead, she belabors her representations, toiling with the tip of her tongue sticking out, and lets her plain hair grow very long, carrying on with this chosen, reclusive lifestyle. I know that the map-maker almost never steps outside, and she sleeps alone, and perseveres seemingly endlessly at a tidy desk in the attic above her modest house.

Out in the world, major travel companies, who had once paid handsomely for the map-maker's maps, confess confusion and criticize her work as "trivial," or "garbled," or "at the very least, inaccurate, and therefore utterly useless." And yet, still, there are a few travelers, albeit very few, who distinguish methods behind the map-maker's madness.

It's all right there, bordered in her shadings, shapes, and lines. Instead of a likeness of what's plainly present, the map-maker's equivocal pictures depict new prospects for highways, fields, mountains, surface streets, and cities at hand. Her Atlas of Abstractions, considered in settings it renders, refers errant travelers to spaces only half-reachable by vehicle, yet informing more fully than a traditional map about the site that is there.

It's as though the map-maker has figured out a way to trace over the experience of the-traveler-in-the-place, instead of merely the place itself, showing not only where one can go, but where one should go, and not even necessarily to get somewhere, instead to go and go.

If Only They Followed the Parables

At the end of the escalator, at the end of the day, on the continuous flattening out of the metal steps, a studious debris has collected. Spun and dumbly pressed against the last landing, repeating dead figures as the steps disappear: colored stubs, wrappers, crushed butts, bags, stained styrofoam cups. Over the stairs, not stopping, turning, they move neither up nor down. The way carries on and cannot take them.

Words Fall Apart

1.

As shattered notes plunge the catchall of silence, urges—gestures—emerge along plot lines spelling *rain*. So it is written. But is to write it to say it? To say that expressions, cast for permanence, transport? Might a port punch through a form, not to express, but to render experience?

To questionable ends, endlessly, an alphabet-spectrum rises daily, one clean shade. From easterly B to highest E, effusive lights of indigo cover every book and earth, above equivocal lids of cloud, to constitute/articulate.

Letters, aflutter, driving from The to A, a determinate range, come to terms. One, glissandi run twenty-six stories, up! Two, hard architectures below the grind begin, ground throughout color. And three, real absence appoints preliminaries: A to Z. If so, there's no telling where letters go without saying.

And the balance? Were it found, we'd hear it denoted entrancing writs of significance, scaled to our knowable, placeable names. Over the total allocation presides (   ). Pronouncing geometries, graduated, (   ) classifies the so-called frame.

2.

April, and all that precipitates.

Delightful shows, light showers, busy raindrops tap like typists, any patter the key to a letter. Skies scroll by in one continuous sheet, typing over, whited out.

What colors commentaries this end of the literal?

A motorhome stopping by, to demonstrate in fields of inclement evenings, signifies Theater. The Chorus, our societal model, engaged in dramatically assertive address, with unnaturally ambiguous voice, bedecked in bells, comes dancing toward us, expressionlessly masked. He or she announces, *our company has emulsified the vernaculars,* then motions to open the windows and doors.

Inside clouded nighttime's chamber void of stars, beneath a rain replacing clouds, under words instead of rain, only lettered, not yet words, a parade has been founded: to play of innocence, stuck in mud-ruts in tall grass, toward one transparent, unquestioning audience? Our parade mustn't founder.

To set the sun, even the sun, among analogies.

(Here was a grain, a definite way the woods went when the woods went, for a moment in effect, necessary to be respected.)

One sequence inevitable, signed like the rest of the past. And periodically more direct, bearing on the heart, borne, a rain more angular than time.

3.

Farther on, beyond, be sheltered, be warm and safe, in a place not yet a place, within a graphic, faded house, you who lives to hear. May a susurrus of light applause come bathe this roof. May a mirror guised as panes replacing windows not confuse. So it's reading verses us in life, and loves the broken letters tame as unnamed sounds. Here, between an M and N, lives my feeling's loud illiteracy.

Or what else do we draw from but belief? Into nightly crimsons jetting, each impending mortality of X, a word, sur-weighted with doubt.

Now, right now, as careful as *I'll hold the nail while you hammer,* with our two kites tied together, peaceful justice-in-love, at the Address of Inclusion we see sentences-to-be, hear martyrdoms with testimonies, spectral letters breathing wisdom's cries, where body parts of songs may weep semantic from the clouds, as phrases offer blossomings: to open things.

Fore

Given shrift. The sun, will it top the leaves? (Musicianly, carried earlyly.) Reroutes the routine.

If factors permit, for just such a . . . piff piff, old bean!

Yes, lets.

Appropriate shimmy, the inexorable next. (Listening . . . for distance.) Airs to hear.

And realified. Me, too!

Then smiles, thanking. By morning, east is still waiting.

Born in Whittier, California, May 25, 1969, raised in Milford, Connecticut, GEOFF BOUVIER holds degrees from The University of Connecticut and from Bard College's Milton Avery Graduate School of the Arts. His chapbook, entitled *Everybody Had a Hat*, won The White Eagle Coffee Store Press Poetry Contest for 2000. He lives in San Diego, where he waits tables at Tapenade Restaurant and publishes journalistic prose with *The San Diego Reader.*

Acknowledgments

Grateful acknowledgment is made to the following publications, where earlier versions of these pieces first appeared:

American Letters & Commentary: A Bee's Advice; The Late Stages of a House-wife

American Poetry Review: Words Fall Apart (as "Word Falls Apart")

Barrow Street: Keep Writing

Blackwater Review: The House in Order

The Café Review: The Opening; Somebody Stop LaSalle

Columbia Poetry Review: Fore

Conduit: Personal Trouble

Dirigible: I Love You! Archaeological Excavation Reveals

Fish Drum: No, No, Never Nothing

Fourteen Hills: The SFSU Review: The Field Clear; Through the Mind

Gargoyle: Organized Philosophy

Hunger: Insert Object Here

Insurance: Metaphysical Ground; New Day Heyday

key satch(el): A Situation; It's All Right Here (as "It's All Right There"); Mission

Lilliput Review: Truth is the Person Who is There

LIT: A Happy Hour

LUNGFULL!: After Measure; Reciprocity Effects

Mudfish: Builder of a Life; Not Pathetic Enough Weather We're Having

New American Writing: Sestina

Noon: A Study of the Common Thing (as "A Study of the Common Moth"); As It Was Going to Be

Oxford Magazine: Fortunate Islands

Paragraph: Secrets of Defense

Pleiades: All Roads Lead

Quarter After Eight: Second Going; Revisionary Traffic (as "Count Your Lover On Both Hands")

Sal Mimeo: Altogether Now; Like the Only Living Thing; The Last Viewpoint; Trying Fire (as "Hot Me"); What is a Subject to Do?

6,500: How to Become a Member

3rd Bed: The Town that Believed Wolf

Tundra: Living Arrangement

Untitled: The Addresses of the Vitalists; Homeless

VOLT: To Speak

West Branch: The Altruist; The Ethics of Tragedy; If Only They Followed the
Parables (as "If They Only Followed the Parables"); Orpheus Out of
Tune; Savings Plan; The Smith Family Trip
Western Humanities Review: Civilization University (as "Civilization 101");
Everybody Had a Hat

The chapbook *Everybody Had a Hat,* published in 2000 by White Eagle Coffee
Store Press, consists of selections from this book.

Also, special thanks to my muses, mentors, friends, and editors, especially:

Kostas Anagnopoulos; Anne Bacon; Durland Barnes; Scott Beal; Courtenay
Bouvier; Jeff Bouvier; Linda Bouvier; Maud Bouvier; Lydia Davis; Peter
Dichsen; Kenji Fujita; Christine Hudman; Jim Holman; Krysia Jopek; Cath
Kane; Jennifer Kane; Ann Lauterbach; MaryAnne Lighty; Nicholas Maw;
Rubi McGrory; Heather McHugh; The Milford "Woodcutters"; Judith Moore;
Marilyn Nelson; Brigitte Noel; Leslie Scalapino; Alexandra Schlein; David
Shapiro; Diane Williams; Pamela DuLong Williams; Suzi Winson; Barbara
Yates.

This couldn't have happened without you.